Dusk Of Life

Neha Garg

India | USA | UK

Made with ❤ on the BookLeaf Publishing Platform
www.bookleafpub.in
www.bookleafpub.com

Dedication

To the gentle hearts that cherish the twilight,
Where shadows dance and silence speak.
To all who find beauty in fleeting moments—
May these verses be a lantern in the dusk of life.

Preface

As the sun dips below the horizon, the world is bathed in hues of fleeting light—moments where endings and beginnings intertwine in silent harmony.

Dusk of Life is a poetic exploration of these in-between spaces, where life's impermanence finds its poetry. The poems reflect on the fragile beauty of existence, capturing the essence of twilight both literal and metaphorical.

In this collection, the poems strive to echo the universality of human emotion—the aching joys, silent heartbreaks, and moments of clarity that come with reflection. It invites readers to pause, to breathe, and to consider how the dusk of life might offer not just closure, but transformation.

I hope these verses stir your soul as deeply as they did mine in their creation.

Acknowledgements

To the quiet moments and twilight skies that whispered
inspiration to my heart,
reminding me that even in endings, there is undeniable
beauty.

Faded Light

Blissful mornings
faded lights
wind in my hair
shadows in my eyes
smile on my lips
and words full of lies
I'm the ruler
I'm the slave
I'm the demon
who slays

Shadow Play

Sunsets are the magic,
spilled across the sky
When shadows dance with light,
Dusk it is
a beautiful maiden,
weaving truth out of lies

Dusk Of Life

Dazed they looked at her
for she was brighter
than the midday sun
and darker
than the midnight sky
They asked who are you
she smiled and spoke
the dusk of life

Untamed

Smirks and shy smiles,
downcast gaze
or staring
with blazing eyes
mischief or sweetness,
or bitter wine
I am who I want to be
Untamed and utterly Wild

Crystal Eyes

If my eyes were crystal,
will the world look
the same,
or will the lies fall
like curtains,
or will the emotions
rain.

Queen Of Cosmos

Her hair tied back
her dress
flowing around,
it was the stars
that she draped
and cosmos
were her crown.

Chamomile

In search for calm
instead of walking for miles,
I reach for my cup of
Chamomile

Dance Of Dead

When I imagined my future
I didn't have broken wings
I wasn't chained and caged
it wasn't the poison running through my veins
It wasn't the sadness I breathed
The chinks in my armour were small dots
not the windows of doom
There still was a heart instead of emptiness
I still was free with wings to fly
Happiness and sunshine were what I breathed
The elixir of life ran through my veins
I wore an armour invincible to defeat
I was alive

But down here buried in this darkness
I am just another corpse
in this cemetery full of
unfulfilled dreams

Paint Me You

Paint me in your color
paint me blue
paint me as if I am sky
paint me like the moon
Paint me new
Paint me you

Ink and Dreams

Inked stain hands
Clothes covered in lint
Dark circles under the eyes
And head full of dreams

This or That

I am not this I am not that
I am something more something else
Something better something worse
An unfinished letter
Or rag in tatters
A flower in bloom
Or a storm of gloom
I am here and I am not
But what I am is what you are not

Beauty

To the rains and blues
Hooded eyes and hues
Lush greens and serene winds
I stay up talking to the moon
Weaving stars on lonely tunes

City Of Dreams

In this city of dream
I am trying to find the real me
There are too many stars
And so are the dreams
So are the faces
And so are the screams
In this loud city
I am trying to find
The real me

Missing Warmth

I woke up again to this miserable life
bleak light and vain pride
Of people being mean and the world being cold
Where the truths are lies and lies are gold
Oh, how I dream of that honey warmth
that melts my heart and light my path
Of joy and laughter and beauty all around
Where people love and not just scowl

Fleeting Images

I sat staring at the blank canvas
images played in front of my eyes
and yet when I picked the brush
they vanished like the last of sunshine.

Like Smoke

I wish I was like smoke,
disappearing and drifting in the wind
I wish I was like dust,
everywhere and nowhere at once
Anywhere but here in this void,
I would love to be
For this waning and waxing like moon
tires the life out of me
This swaying like tides
rising and falling
drains the energy of my storms
I want to burst like cosmos
creating and destroying
instead of this black hole
Eternally falling.

Letters To The Sky

To the sky that is sleeping
a restless heart writes
about the wonders it holds
locked in its mind

Sparks

She's made of needle and flowers,
of dreams and reality
and fire and sparks

Of swords and pens
of philosophical bends and realistic mends
glitter and stars
she is peace she is war

Infinite

Bones made of stardust
sunlight in my veins
Tresses of dark night
constellations are my name
Body made of stone
and touch featherlight
Ocean is my gaze
Siren song is my voice

Tangled

My words are river
Churning and flowing,
endless is the abyss
in which it falls
I wonder where their shores echo
crashing like forgotten dreams
Tangled in the roots of memory
snared in someone else's reach
or floating unchecked
endlessly

The Weaver

Pen gliding on paper
like boats rocking in the sea
The stories are storms
that drowns you and me
Woven are dreams
with sweet sugar spun clouds
Syrupy are the lakes
with boats made of floral crowns
Dungeons and dragons
and skyscrapers alike
I rule I run I play with vice
Imagination wild
and sweet notes that pull
I put my pen to paper
to weave a world new and full

The Eternal Hunt

To the weaver of storms
those ride lightning and winds
wild are their manes
that holds galaxies still
The universe stops and stares
when they breath constellations to life
untamed are their souls
that are sunshine lined
They are what stories are born of
creatures of dreams and night
They are sweet melodies
that brings horrors to life
they are melancholy
they are joy
they are springs of youth
and rivers spry
twirling and weaving
between spaces
like day and night